We see our boat.

We're on the boat.

The anchor's up.

We wave goodbye.

The boat goes out.

We're far away.

We see a tanker.

It is big.

We see a sailboat.

We see a fishing boat.

We see a cargo ship.

We see an ocean liner.

We see a tail.

Wow!

We see the whale.